To: Lance Corpal Brian Edgar
Semper Fi and best wishes
David C. Milam
2-26-05

The Last Bomb

A U.S. Marine's Memoirs of Nagasaki

David C. Milam

EAKIN PRESS ◆ Austin, Texas

For CIP
information,
please access:
www.loc.gov

FIRST EDITION
Copyright © 2001
By David C. Milam
Published in the United States of America
By Eakin Press
A Division of Sunbelt Media, Inc.
P.O. Drawer 90159 ⌨ Austin, Texas 78709-0159
email: eakinpub@sig.net
🖥 website: www.eakinpress.com 🖥
ALL RIGHTS RESERVED.

1   2   3   4   5   6   7   8   9

1-57168-659-2 HB
1-57168-627-4 PB

Contents

Acknowledgments

It never occurred to me that I had a story to tell—somehow it was just a part of a war that happened several wars ago. There was nothing heroic that I did, nor did anything happen to me that didn't also happen to many other American servicemen in that part of the world.

But then I met three gentlemen at a military antiques show in 1997—Bill Kilpatrick, Robert Grayson, and Harry Akers. When, in our discussion, the subject of the atomic bomb came up, I told them something of my remembrances of its effects on Nagasaki, as I was stationed there soon after the blast. Mr. Kilpatrick, president of Texas Militia Collectors Association, encouraged me to put these memories on paper, as did Mr. Grayson and Mr. Akers. The enthusiasm of these men, with their vast knowledge of war history, made me wonder if I had something significant to share.

My wife Beverly has offered unending support, as has Pam Sitler, the wife of my long-time friend and deer-hunting partner John Sitler. Pam has really picked up the pieces to help a guy who doesn't know the first thing about writing a book. I've also taken the liberty of asking numerous close friends to read the manuscript. I received great input, and for that I thank you all, especially Jim Lowe, Charlie Payne, Dan and Mary B. Hayslett, Ollie Schaetter, Dayton Hahne, and Fred Hirschler. A special thanks goes to Ed Robbins and Steve Hardy, who found some great research material on the Internet, and very grateful thanks to Wanda and Cliff Hahne, who found Robin Hardy, editor of this book.

Preface

What was Nagasaki like after the atom bomb? When I first viewed the devastation that killed 73,000 out of a population of 240,000, I was reminded of Jesus' comment to his disciples as they were admiring the temple buildings: "There shall not be left here one stone upon another that shall not be thrown down." It was total destruction.

The information in this account is drawn mostly from my memory of events fifty-three years ago. Some things you never forget. I become a little irritated when young people confuse World War II with the first world war, or worse, with Korea or Vietnam. The ignorance tends to take the edge off our hard-won victory over Japan. I wonder if anyone considers what it would have been like had the Japanese become the victors—and our dictators!

Many accounts of the War in the Pacific have been documented, but I have not seen much on the occupation of Japan and the aftermath of the war. This is not surprising, because we tend to go on with our lives, to try to forget the horrors of the past. But we need to remember. We need to understand.

Basically, my account covers events preliminary to and during my duty at the site of the detonation of the atom bomb in Nagasaki. Photographs that have never before been published are included here. I think that they alone tell the story better than I ever could.

Private First Class David Milam upon completion of boot camp, January 1944.

CHAPTER ONE

Camp and Code Talkers

A boot camp morning started with reveille at 4:30 A.M. The wake-up call on a worn-out record was played over large speakers mounted over the tent area. You could hardly tell what the sound was supposed to be—it came close to two wildcats fighting during mating season—but every single man responded.

It rained a lot in California, a cold rain. One night it rained continuously, all night long. We were, as usual, exhausted from the rigors of the day. When the miserable screeching of reveille emanated from the cold, rainy darkness to beat on the dead ears of men slumbering in leaking tents, it had no effect. The next sound we were conscious of was the piercing voice of our drill instructor (DI) yelling, "Hit the deck, you shit birds! Hit it NOW!"

The warm blankets covered with ponchos flew off, and our feet hit the ground, so to speak. It was covered with six to eight inches of cold rainwater. Our shoes, which had been carefully placed beneath our cots in military fashion, had floated all over the tent with their cargo of wet socks. You can imagine the chaos as we splashed and groped for our shoes in the dark, for we "boots" had no lights in our tents. Meanwhile, there were three DIs screaming obscenities at us for our lack of immediate response to roll call. Yeah, we got dressed down for that, big time.

And we must have looked like a bunch of sad-sack Marines, standing in various dress, ankle-deep in mud, some with one shoe, others with no shoes, all soaking wet and shivering, under one lighted post for roll call and inspection. It was November 1943.

On July 23 of that year I had turned eighteen years of age. I was somewhat disgruntled that my parents had refused to sign a waiver that would have allowed me to join the military before then. World War II was going hot and heavy at the time, and even though there was no real assurance that we would win, the urge to get in the thick of things was gnawing at me more and more with each passing day. Although it may sound crazy today, I was afraid that the war would end before I could do my part in *Gung Ho* with John Wayne and company! The preceding January, I had gone to the draft board to remind them that I would be eighteen in July. I was packed and ready.

I didn't receive my draft notice until October, and was sworn in by late November. Patriotism was at an all-time high. Anyone who attempted to dodge the draft was the lowest of the low, in the country's way of thinking.

At last I was on my way to the United States Marine Corps Recruit Depot in San Diego, California. Little by little, my new world began to take shape. Marine Corps boot camp was nothing like the movies. The term is derived from Basic Training, which lasted eight weeks. Its purpose was to acquaint us with all aspects of military life—rifle handling, hygiene, fitness, hardships, alertness, taking orders, marching, and guard duty. The idea was to whip us into shape ASAP—and filter out the unfit. Anyone with corporal stripes was next to a general as far as a "boot" was concerned. Discipline was driven home with the firmness of a sledgehammer.

During the first days of boot training, we were massed together in what looked like a boxing ring, with bleachers on all sides so that everyone could get a clear view. Several high-ranking officers stood in the center to talk to us about what would be expected in combat. Their question was, Could you kill another man? And, if you could not bring yourself to do it, why not?

No one responded at first, then one of the officers assured the crowd that no harm would come to anyone who, for whatever reason, would not carry out this act of war. Finally, some hands went up. As best as I can remember, some of the reasons voiced were: it was against their religious beliefs; they were conscientious objectors; they just couldn't kill another person. I felt that some who said this were looking for a way out of the military. If they were, they were disappointed, because we found out they would serve as stretcher bearers. I believe this was worse than anything, as the enemy showed no regard for a helmet with a red cross. It just made the man wearing it a more obvious target.

Then the Navy doctors had one-on-one talks with each of us, and began to ask questions like, Do you like girls? Did you ever have sex with a girl? And how do you feel about men? Well, to be honest, I was just not that worldly. I thought the doctor who was asking me all these questions was just plain sick. It made me glad that I had not elected to serve in the Navy.

A form of flu hit just about every man. We referred to it as "cat fever." If you turned into sick bay and were out of commission for a few days, then you were reassigned to a new platoon and your training started all over again from ground zero. However, if you could stick it out sick as a horse, then you could graduate with the platoon you started with. You learned real fast that bitching got you nowhere. This was just part of the training to change boys into men, according to Marine Corps tradition.

After two months of boot camp, we were ready for line camp, where we would receive specialized training prior to combat. We were informed that Camp Joseph H. Pendleton, which covered more than 100,000 acres in California, would be the training grounds for the newly formed 5th Marine Division.[1] Most of us were eighteen or younger, and from the southern part of the country, primarily Texas.

At line camp, more men joined us

from the Marine Corps Base in Quantico, Virginia. We were to be trained as artillery men on 105 howitzers (field artillery). There were three batteries in each battalion, plus H&S (Headquarters and Services Department). Each battery consisted of four howitzers and about 250 men. The three batteries in our battalion were K, L, and M; I was in L. At this time, I requested to be in motor transport, where I would be trained on all vehicles. Being in L battery, I gave the Jeep I was assigned a name beginning with that letter—"Liberty Hound." This Jeep, true to its name, would prove a valuable companion later on. Like all drivers, I had a secondary job as a replacement on the gun crew.

Then a few more men joined each battery—Indians from the Navajo reservation. At that time, we had no idea of the important role these Indians were to play in communications as "code talkers." They were training to transmit messages in their native tongue, which could not be decoded by outsiders, because it was unlike any other language.

I can recall only one name of the three Navajo Indians who were in my platoon—Murphy. (He is second from left on the first row of the group picture.) Not an Indian name, I believe. They were not very friendly and stayed together most of the time. Murphy was one of the eight men in my tent during boot training. He seemed to take all of this white man's army in stride, without a lot to say—that is, until one cold, rainy morning when we were all jammed in the head (bathroom) to shave and get ready for roll call. We were given five minutes to do all of this with about six washbasins for sixty men.

When Murphy's turn came up, he was going through the motions of shaving when one of our DIs, Private First

Class Demeter, noticed that there was no blade in Murphy's razor. When Demeter began to raise hell, Murphy tried to explain that Indian boys pluck all of their facial hair as they mature. It was a tradition among the Navajos, and most every other tribe, as far as he knew. Not only would shaving encourage the growth of whiskers (which they did not want), but it may have been contrary to their religious beliefs.

Anyway, Murphy stood up to Demeter and told him to throw him in the brig if he wanted, but neither he nor the other two Navajos were going to shave. It was a brave act. I don't know what discussions took place after the Navajos were taken to the brig, but they were back the next day "shaving" without razor blades.

The Indian next to last on the first row of the group picture could only speak a few words of English, so almost everything had to be interpreted for him by the other two. I will never know how this little guy got in the Marine Corps, because he could hardly see beyond his rifle barrel. We were given all sorts of physicals, so anything as noticeable as this should have been red-flagged right away. I wondered at the time if they thought he was trying to fake his way out.

We were taken to a preliminary firing range where .22-caliber rifles were used for target practice. The space allowed for each man was absurd—we were so close together that our shoulders were almost touching. The targets were correspondingly crammed together so that it was difficult to tell which one was yours. This Indian, when he began shooting, hit everything but the target, but the fellow next to him, Private Hawk, was a pretty good shot and put all his rounds in the Indian's bull's-eye! The

DIs were now more convinced than ever that the Indian could see just fine. It was not until several months into line camp that he was given a medical discharge. Since he had such a good command of the Navajo language, it is my belief that the code talkers were hoping to keep him regardless of his eyesight.

One pivotal event involving the code talkers had to do with the flag-raising on Mt. Suribachi on Iwo Jima, which became famous as the defining moment of the victory over Japan. As the American flag was raised, the code talkers relayed this information in Navajo. The code was translated by matching up the first letter of each English word corresponding to each Navaho word, hence: *dibeh* (sheep), *no-dah-ih* (Ute), *gah* (rabbit), *tkin* (ice), *shush* (bear), *wol-la-chee* (ant), *moasi* (cat), *lin* (horse), *yeh-hes* (itch). The message relayed in this manner was, Suribachi is secured.[2]

Navajo was useful for many reasons, but especially in its dissimilarity to English. The language as used by the code talkers was entirely verbal—nothing was written. And it may require an entire sentence in English, including descriptives, to translate a single Navajo word. Since there were no words for names of modern armaments in Navajo, the code talkers substituted names of plants and animals. The Navajo word *ch'al* (frog) translated to "amphibious operation;" *ni-ma-si* (potatoes) meant "grenades;" *a-ye-shi* (eggs) were "bombs;" and *nihima* (our mother) was "America." The war intelligence department of our enemy in the Pacific, the Japanese, was hard to fool. They had broken many American codes. Therefore, if Navajo could trip them up, it would prove invaluable. Sure enough, the Japanese never broke it.

One major drawback to this system was the heavy radio equipment that had to be packed and carried on the back of some poor Marine—the code talker—making him the natural target of enemy fire. According to Marine signal officer Major Howard Conner, code talkers transmitted more than 800 messages on Iwo Jima alone. It was his assessment that had it not been for them, the number of casualties would have been much greater. The Navajos were awarded special medallions for their contribution to ending the war, but not until June of 1969.[3]

Boot camp graduation picture. Private First Class. Milam is on the third row from the top, third from the left, looking down. The Navajo code talkers are on the first row, second from left (Murphy), ninth and tenth from left.

The #4 gun crew at Camp Pendleton, California, enjoying a beer party before shipping out. The arrow indicates the first sergeant; Milam is kneeling at the sergeant's right.

Pfc. J. B. Jones of Houston, Texas, and Pfc. D. C. Milam of Dallas, Texas, proudly pose with one of the twelve 105 Howitzers that composed their 13th Marine Regiment.

Pictured here is the motor transport team of drivers for the "L" Battery, referred to as "Love" Battery, which is a part of the Morse Code. The trucks were used to tow the guns and ammo. The Jeeps were for scout, forward observers, captains, or general purposes.

1. Pfc. Allen Rose
2. Cpl. Jim Rogers
3. Pfc. William Holly
4. Pfc. Lee Whitmer

5. Pvt. Wilber Suba
6. Cpl. Robert Alderman
7. Pfc. Ivan Taylor
8. Sft. Wilber Redic

9. Pfc. Gerald Sharp
10. Pfc. Carl Johnson
11. Pfc. Hollis Stringer
12. Pfc. David Milam

13. Cpl. Thomas Matthews
14. Pvt. Earl Fletcher
15. Pfc. Frank Rychel
16. 1st Lt. Stanley Sumner

CHAPTER TWO

Brig Rat

On July 4, 1944, we were ordered to turn in our M-1 Garand rifles in exchange for M-1 carbine rifles, as the latter were better suited for artillery mobility than the larger Garand infantry rifles. We were to take our newly issued weapons to the firing range to become more familiar with them. Each man was given fifty rounds of ammo, and the firing began. Some of us were ordered to leave our rifles on the firing stake for the cooks and messmen to use, as they had not yet received theirs. All ammunition had to be exhausted before returning to camp. A private first class named Eisenlore used my rifle and returned it to me supposedly empty of cartridges.

Because the new rifles were a little stiff, the bolts did not reliably fit all the way into the receiver to eject the shell. A gunnery sergeant was in charge of checking to see that no live shells remained in the chamber when we were through. He had spent many years in the Marines and followed the rules to the letter. Little did I know he was about to miss one.

Rifle inspection immediately followed our firing practice. I opened the bolt on my rifle and the chamber cleared, leaving the weapon cocked and, unfortunately, still loaded. Worst of all, it went totally undetected by myself and the inspecting officer.

We reboarded the artillery trucks, which began heading back to the barracks. While my mind was back in Dallas, my finger was on the trigger of my rifle, which lay across my lap, pointing at the floorboard of the truck. For some undetermined reason—a sudden memory, an unconscious reflex, a lurch of the truck—I squeezed the trigger. The explosion that followed seemed unreal. Wood flew up from the deck, and everyone was craning to see the hole in the floor. Then the same man who had used my rifle discovered that there was a hole in his right foot as well. Although he hadn't felt it, the bullet had passed right through his instep. A trail of blood began to follow his shoe wherever he moved it.

He must have thought he was dying, because he turned pale and began yelling, "I've been hit! I've been hit!" A corporal new to our battery was a seasoned fighting man who thought he knew just what to do. He took the rifle sling and began to twist it around Eisenlore's ankle, thinking it would stop the bleeding until we got to sick bay. Unfortunately, the rifle sling pinched the hell out of his ankle while doing nothing for the bleeding wound.

Just six months in the Marines, and I had shot one of our own guys. In camp, yet. Since it was unintentional and not entirely my fault, I hoped punishment would not be too severe. WRONG, Jirene! It was taken very seriously indeed. I would be court-martialed.

A man I will call Lieutenant Noteworthy was assigned as my defense attorney, although he was not an attorney. Marine Corps law—The Rocks and Shoals—saw fit to have me represented by an officer. What a joke! Lieutenant Noteworthy met with me and said, "Look, I'm going to tell you like it is. If you really wish to contest this court-martial, then it would behoove you to hire a civilian attorney familiar with the by-laws of the Marine Corps. He will ask for a general court-martial, so that it would be necessary to go to a higher court. It would be expensive, and your transfer to another unit would be necessary. Besides, I can't really help you, because they want to make an example of you. I would be fighting the system, which would go hard on me. My suggestion to you is just to plead guilty and bite the bullet. The gunnery sergeant who was in charge at the firing range is not going to be held responsible, even though he missed the round in his inspection. He is a twenty-year man, and punishment for him would be disgraceful." Lieutenant Noteworthy was at that time with H&S, but he and I were to see more of each other later on. Needless to say, I bit the bullet.

As Lieutenant Noteworthy had promised, I was held up as a perfect example of the dangers of carelessness to the rest of my newly formed division. I was ordered to stand before our entire battalion on the steps of the Chow Hall at noon two days later. There, I was dressed down and given a summary court-martial. My punishment was thirty days on bread and water in solitary confinement in the division brig.

Up to this point, I had been very proud of being a Marine and had accepted all discipline and regimentation in stride. Now I could have died of shame.

About four days later, I was on my way to the stockade under armed guard. I felt life was not worth living. I was a disgrace to everyone. What would I tell my parents? No one in my family had ever been incarcerated for anything! I was a "brig rat." Some of my friends even shunned me. In a desperate effort to keep this news from my family, I wrote them a letter to the effect that I would be on special manuevers for thirty days and could not write them.

The worst was yet to come. I arrived at the stockade early in the morning. It was surrounded by high barbed-wire fences and four armed guard towers. My belongings were put in a locker, and I was given dungarees that had a large yellow "P" painted on the back and front. My head was shaved, and I was given a pith helmet to wear. (The helmets, part of the prison garb, were to shield our bare heads from the hot sun.) I was not allowed to speak to anyone, nor receive mail or phone calls. Although I was incarcerated, my time did not start right away. The solitary confinement cells were full because so many men had gone AWOL after returning home from combat. There was a two- to three-week wait for a "suite." I was to live in a tent with eight other prisoners and go out on work parties during the day until a cell became available.

The very next morning, we lined up at prisoner attention: arms folded straight out. Our indoctrination came from a fat Marine first sergeant who looked unkempt and smelled of old booze. Mean as hell, he proceeded to let us know that our souls might belong to God, but our asses belonged to the Marine Corps brig.

Then he inspected each man. We were to call out name, rank, and serial number as he passed in front of us. He came to a stop about every fourth or fifth man, called him a bastard (with descriptives), and kicked him in the shin. When the man bent over in pain, the sergeant slapped his head, causing the pith helmet to go flying. Then two other NCOs (noncommissioned officers) who were part of the inspection team roughed these men up and put them back in formation. I was sweating bullets as he passed me. He did not stop, because I quickly discerned the secret: not to make eye contact with him.

We began our work detail, which was picking up the division's trash on garbage trucks. Four prisoners with two armed guards were assigned to each truck. This went on for two long weeks. I was becoming bitter and more mindful of looking out for me first.

Then one day we were sent to the Marine women's headquarters to pick up their garbage. We were doing our thing when a woman's voice rang out: "David Milam, is that you?"

It was a girl I had known in the town where I had grown up—Emma Lou Gary from Vicksburg, Mississippi. I acted as though I had not heard her and

kept my back to her until the slow truck rambled out of her sight. At this moment I sank to the depths of whale dung, hating the whole Marine Corps.

Finally, my solitary confinement cell was ready. It was five feet wide and seven feet long, with a cement floor and heavy wire mesh covering the top about eight feet overhead. Crossing each cell was a catwalk where a guard would periodically make his rounds. At sundown, I was given two blankets, which were taken away promptly at 5:00 A.M. There was nothing else in the cell—no bunk, no nothing. When one person needed restroom facilities, no matter what time of the day or night, every one of us had to make formation and march to the head (outdoor bathroom) and take care of business with the turnkey (guard) screaming at us the entire way. With two hundred men, this was a continuous thing.

Each meal consisted of four slices of bread and one cup of water. On the third day we received all three meals, a full ration for that day. At first we stuffed ourselves, but learned this would only make us sick. Also on the third day, we could treat ourselves to a cold shower and brush our teeth. Once.

There were times when I thought I was losing it. I kept myself occupied by making marks on the wooden planks with my thumbnail to keep track of the time as it crawled by. In between the cracks of the two-by-six-inch plank wall, I lined up the flies and mosquitos that I had become quite agile in snaring.

At 5:00 A.M., a turnkey came to the cell door, which was locked from the outside with a horseshoe-shaped drop latch. If a man was still lying down, he would be roused with a kick to the feet and a shouted obscenity. I had a corner cell that was next to the desk where the guards talked and ate all night long. I could see them through the cracks, and my stomach would drive me nuts! I could also see some of the prisoners who had gotten in trouble with the guards. Their punishment was to be handcuffed to the overhead catwalk by each wrist so that their feet would barely touch the deck. When they got tired of standing and hung their weight on the cuffs, it would eventually cut their wrists. The guards had absolutely no feeling for anyone there. I saw a lot of shoving and kicking.

One day the cell next to mine was emptied, and almost immediately a new body was impounded. I promptly checked him out through the crack in my cell. He was a wiry guy with three or four days' growth of beard. I could smell the alcohol on his breath, as my nose had become as sharp as a bloodhound's. He had a scar that went the entire length of one side of his face. This guy looked like he belonged right where he was! The next morning the guards started their procedure of opening the cells, and when the guard kicked the newcomer, he grabbed the turnkey in a death grip and took his sidearm. The other guards who heard the scuffling arrived to meet a .45 automatic staring them in the face.

Some serious discussion took place, and the prisoner gave up the gun only after insisting that they call his commanding officer, who happened to be Lieutenant Colonel Carlson. This was the same Colonel Carlson of the famous Carlson's Raiders. He led them on the most dangerous forays, like surprise attacks behind enemy lines and forward advances from submarines. They were some real tough characters—what an attitude! I had watched their training once and never saw anything that compared to their way of warfare.

Later that day, Colonel Carlson arrived at the stockade. He was not friendly, especially to the grizzled old first sergeant who ran the brig. Carlson was firm and demanding. He got his man out of the brig without so much as paperwork, as far as I could tell. I only wished that my commanding officer would have stood up for me half as much.[1]

Time was nearing for my release. Then one day I was taken to the main prison quarters and told that I had a letter to read and answer. It was from my parents. They had learned the truth after calling my CO, Capt. Richard Jeske. Their letter was to assure me that I was not disgraced, and that they thought more of me for trying to keep them from worrying. It nearly tore my heart out.

One late afternoon we were all marched out to the open area inside the stockade compound. There, a master sergeant whom we had not seen before pitched us an offer: they would release from the brig any man who was willing to join the next combat mission, and the offense for which we were incarcerated would be stricken from our records. Why the generous attitude? Because it was likely that our part of the mission would be infantry—first wave into combat. He made no bones about it: the odds were not favorable. He then asked that anyone who wanted immediate release on these terms to step forward.

I was surprised at how many men stepped out of rank. If it had not been so close to my release, I would have been tempted to join them. But I remained in rank while still more men came forward.

It was not too long afterward that the invasion of Guam took place. The casualty lists that came back from that battle were awesome. The numbers mounted daily, especially among the first wave who were pinned down on the beachhead. Needless to say, I was relieved that I had not made the impulsive decision to go.[2]

At last, after forty-five days, I was released from the brig, fifteen pounds less than the one hundred fifty I weighed when I went in. Captain Jeske met with me first thing to tell me more about the conversation with my parents and to welcome me back. I was supposed to have been transferred to another unit, but he stepped in and kept me as his driver. I'm sure he meant it as an honor, or a show of trust, but I would just as soon have passed. From that day on, I went about my duties with a shade less enthusiasm than before.

Private First Class Milam with his faithful friend in trouble, the Liberty Hound.

Shipping Out!

As line-camp training got underway, we received still more personnel into the 5th Marine Division. They were seasoned Marines who had seen tough fighting all the way back from Guadalcanal.[1] They not only had scars from combat, but strange diseases such as malaria, jungle rot, and elephantiasis. On rare occasions, we would hear of their experiences, in which torture and slow death figured heavily. I am sure these inspirational sessions were meant to be part of our training.

Since most of us were at a very impressionable age, we saw our role as U.S. Marines as a "real big deal," especially if we wanted to become a real "salt"—a seasoned Marine with a chest full of ribbons, among them the Purple Heart, the most treasured possession a man could possibly have.

Fortunately, the war never reached American soil (except for the Gulf intrusions, but more on that later). Yet it definitely had its effects on conveniences that most of us take for granted. Many staples, such as food items, gasoline, and auto parts, were rationed. No new cars were manufactured for civilian use, nor were stoves, refrigerators, cameras, or anything remotely similar to products used in war.

While we were in line camp at Pendleton, cameras were permitted as long as field maneuvers were not photographed. A few of the men would take pictures of our battery from time to time, and I thought it would be great to do likewise. My parents had an old box camera that was outdated even then, having been made in the early thirties. But it did work, and it was not their primary camera, so I asked them to send it to me, which they did. I took photographs of my buddies, guns, trucks, and everything that we were so proud of—after all, we were the best—which I sent home.

I knew that the time was drawing near for our overseas departure, so I stocked up on film that was available at the PX (store for military personnel only). We had already been advised that no cameras were to leave the country, but this could not include *me*, as I had visions of getting some real war action pictures, like those we saw in training films and the newsreels back home. This idiotic reasoning could have landed me in San Quentin, but my guardian angel must have been watching over me as I stashed the camera and film in my sea bag. That poor, antiquated camera—and the film!—wound up traveling several thousands of miles in the hot holds of several ships with very little damage. Our sea bags got lost, and we were issued new sea bags with everything they had contained. Then, a year later, they mysteriously turned up again—mine with camera and film intact.

Finally, line-camp training at Pendleton was completed. The "Old Man," our skipper, Captain Jeske (who was at least twenty-five) announced those graceful words from the Wallace Beery/John Wayne movies: "Okay, men, this is it!" His fist was held proud and high. "Get ready for what we were trained to do! *We are shipping out!*"[2]

Our response was instant: all whooping and hollering. That night we were allowed to purchase two beers at the Slop Chute, the beer garden. All liberties were cancelled. We were to have no contact with the outside world for the time being.

As I recall, three weeks passed, and then we were on our way aboard a very overcrowded troop transport, heading who knew where! The second day at sea we heard an alarm that sounded like a Model A Ford—*Auuga! Auuga!* Then a voice over the loudspeaker announced, "This is not a drill! All hands below deck!" It suddenly occurred to me that this would be a hell of a way to die, four decks below without a single shot fired at the enemy—without even a sight of them! We were not told at the time, but the alert was because an enemy subma-rine had been picked up on our radar. Our bunks were the only place to retreat. They were stacked eight high, so close together that you couldn't turn over. You slept on either your back or your stomach, period.

Because the ship's hull smelled so foul (due to overcrowding), I was very anxious to go topside each morning, which I did very early because only a certain number of men were allowed on deck at once. One morning I was enjoying the fresh sea air when I suddenly noticed that two narrow ships were headed straight toward us. As they approached, I could see that they were U.S. Navy destroyers, and they passed our ship very quickly on either side. When they were about a mile past us, I could see columns of water rise from their depth charges. A Japanese sub had tried to position itself for a shot with a tin fish—a torpedo—at us. Of course, we were never informed as to what became of the sub.

Land could be sighted in the far distance. It turned out to be our beachhead, Pearl Harbor. As we made our approach toward the entrance, all men were ordered topside to view the graveyard of our Navy, courtesy of the Japanese surprise attack two and a half years earlier.[3] It was a dramatic moment as we passed the rusty remains of the mighty battlewagons laid to rest in the harbor. All men were at attention to salute the dead still entombed in the ships' hulls. Taps was sounded in the background. I am sure a surge of hatred went through most of us. The cement docks still bore the scars of war. Oil slicks still oozed from the sunken vessels across the water of the passageway to our docking area. We were not allowed to go ashore, because we were to set sail early the next day.

This trip was short. We landed on the big island at Hilo, Hawaii, and then were transported in cattle cars to the top of the rock, where an old tent area had been prepared. This was Camp Tarawa, where the 2nd Marine Division had taken its training prior to the Tarawa Invasion.[4] Of all the beautiful places that Hawaii had to offer, this was the pits! Lava rock and fine dust whipped about by generous winds were all we saw every day. We stayed filthy, as we had nothing but cold water to shower and wash clothes in. This place resembled many of the enemy-held islands. Maybe our leaders knew what they were doing, after all!

Training was intense, and so was discipline. It seemed as though we would wear out the 105 howitzers before we really needed them. Many men complained of deafness from the noise of the blasts, even though our ears were stuffed with cotton. All of our outgoing mail was read and censored by our own staff, and our letters were cut to the point of absurdity. In some instances, those letters were a way for us to let off steam without being called on the carpet for insubordination. Because we were isolated from the world, we never knew for sure how the war was going. On rare occasions, we would be called on to transport supplies to the Naval Air Station in Hilo. The big thrill was to get to see a few nurses, who were, of course, surrounded by officers, majors, and higher-ups.

One amusing incident occurred when I drove Captain Jeske and Lieutenant Stewart to Hilo for a USO function. As we passed a couple of Navy WAVES (Women Accepted for Volunteer Emergency Service), Captain Jeske nudged me: "Milam, pull up to those girls—see if they need a ride or something."

"I'll do better than that, Skipper," I promised, a rash, green eighteen-year-old kid. Whereupon I did a U-turn and pulled up alongside the startled women. I hopped out of the Jeep, tipped my hat, and said, "Ladies, I'm in desperate trouble, and if you'd be so kind to help me, I'd be forever grateful."

They looked at each other, and one asked, "What is it?" Skipper and the lieutenant had no idea where I was going with this.

"Ladies, my whole military career is hanging in the balance. You see, my superior officers here do not wish to go to the USO show unescorted. If you would graciously consent to go with them, that would make my career—commendations, decorations, probably even a promotion. If you won't, it's liable to be the stockade for me. Will you please help me out here?" This was particularly cheeky, as a Pfc. was unfit to even address a Navy WAVE. Had they taken offense, I could have gotten in real trouble.

One started to laugh and walk off, but the other said, "Hey, why not?" So they agreed. I gave the skipper the keys to the Jeep feeling like I had won the war right there.

For sanitation purposes, because of the filth we lived in, the Navy doctors issued a once-in-a-lifetime offer for the men who had not been circumcised—in one day and out the next evening. We had a Sergeant Reddic, not the most popular NCO in our battery, who participated in this operation. Following his surgery, one of our favorite pastimes was to tell sexy stories anytime he was around. We hoped he'd pull a few stitches. He did walk kind of funny for a while after that.

Once in a while, the radio operator who manned the Jeep that housed the radio equipment, Corporal Jones, would allow a few of us to listen in to Tokyo Rose.[5] This was definitely a forbidden activity, and Corporal Jones had to be very selective as to who was invited to listen. Tokyo Rose's broadcasts, beamed to U.S.-held islands, were filled with de-moralizing lies about the slaughtering of U.S. troops and how our wives and girl-friends were cheating on us. She came up with the actual names of individual Marines and some of our positions in the Pacific, which were supposed to be se-cret. She claimed to have spies among us. There must have been some truth to that, because many Japanese descendants inhabited Hawaii, and many of them couldn't even speak English. On numer-ous occasions, our tower guards ob-served blinking lights from the sur-rounding mountainsides, which were ac-knowledged by others along the coastal areas where Japanese subs were reported to be surfacing at night.[6]

The war seemed so far away. Our closest encounter with the enemy at this point had been a solitary Jap sub that was following our troop transport to Hawaii. One night during one of our many field maneuvers, our battalion of twelve guns was within just a few miles of the Pacific shoreline overlooking the ocean when the moon made itself visible. All precau-tions of combat alert were being ob-served as usual, which required us to wear full camouflage and prohibited smoking, flashlights, vehicle lights, and loud noises. Most of us regarded this as just routine until our artillery began fir-ing at a submarine that had surfaced within reach of our guns (with a range of seven miles). As soon as our artillery had determined the sub's position, all guns were in full operation. The only time we

could see it was when the moon came briefly into view from behind the clouds. If we did not hit the sub, we sure came close. It either submerged on its own, or with our assistance. Of course, we were never informed which it was.

The European theater seemed to get most of the talent who entertained the troops overseas. I guess this was be-cause our troops in the Pacific were scat-tered over many miles of tiny islands, most of which were in dangerous war zones. But while we were still at Camp Tarawa, Hawaii, a good-news message was passed along to us by our command-ing officer. We were informed that the Red Cross was going to establish a post staffed by Red Cross girls. Their func-tion was to help raise morale among the troops by passing out doughnuts on oc-casion, playing cards with us, and just chatting with us in general (no dancing).

So we built their living quarters, cleaned their barracks every day, posted heavy guard duty around their com-pound, and did their laundry. Also, we chauffeured them around while they dated the officers and drew big overseas pay. This short-lived arrangement did nothing to help our morale or the war ef-fort. The Red Cross girls were not only personally unpopular among the troops, but soured our impression of that whole organization.

Then, in early February 1945, we were ordered to load ship. This time it was different. We worked around the clock nonstop for seven days and seven nights as we again headed into the un-known.

CHAPTER FOUR

Surrender

On February 19, 1945, at 1:59 A.M., Task Force 58 of the 5th and 4th Marine divisions began landing an assault on the tiny island of Iwo Jima, the gateway to Tokyo. Three days later, we were joined by elements of the 3rd Marine division. We stormed the beach under withering fire. It was just like maneuvers—only now they were shooting back. The Japanese had built miles of tunnels and concrete pillboxes all over the island that could only be neutralized by a direct hit. The only way to take the island was a rock at a time.[1]

After thirty-six days of bitter fighting, the island was declared secured. The cost to the Marine Corps was the highest casualty rate in its 168-year history: 5,931 killed and 19,920 wounded. Additional casualties from the Army, Navy, and Seabees were 2,835, bringing the total to 28,686 killed or wounded.[2]

The 5th Marine Division returned to Camp Tarawa once more. A very definite change had taken place among the men. I have never seen such widespread personality change. The eighteen-year-olds who were now twenty seemed suddenly more somber and definitely more mature.

Germany surrendered.[3] The war was beginning to make sense—but why were the Japanese still hanging on? Their only possession was their home islands of Japan. Their navy and air power were nonexistent, but we knew they would fight to the very last man, and in so doing, cost us dearly. Their homeland defense was incredibly strong.

On August 16, 1945, word came that Hiroshima had been devastated by our new weapon, the atomic bomb. This had to be the end. We started betting on how soon it would be before we could return home. But when the Imperial Japanese government refused to answer our demands or meet with our government, it made us wonder if this weapon was as powerful as we were led to believe. Then word came that a second A-bomb drop had been made over Nagasaki.[4] The Japanese officials responded a little better this time, finally surrendering.[5]

We were, as usual, having another field maneuver in the dust bowl when our Jeep radio crackled that the war was over; the Japanese had finally given up—maybe. Every dust-covered Marine was all smiles. All you could see under all that dust were the whites of our eyes and our teeth. Our battalion commander ordered each battery to expend all ammunition by firing at will, and then wrap it up for the day. Unfortunately, the war had not ended for us. During the rapid-fire operation, one of the battalion's guns rocked off its line of fire, and the shells landed on the 27th Marine Infantry Regiment, killing five or six men and wounding even more. The 26th, 27th, and 28th Marine Regiments of the 5th Division had all suffered more than 100 percent casualties on Iwo Jima (that is, all the original members were either killed or wounded, then replacements were killed or wounded). They didn't deserve this terrible mistake. Since we could not determine whose gun was off target, we all returned to camp in a state of depression when we should have been rejoicing over the war's end.

The invasion of Japan came first, then the occupation, because no one could be sure that the Japanese would really surrender. We loaded ship once more.[6] This time there was no doubt as to where we were going. We were armed to the teeth, ready for the worst. We sailed to Saipan,[7] our ship dropping anchor about dusk. There, on top of a very high cliff, was a village where some Japanese women, children, and old people still lived. Some of the Navy personnel told us that it was called "Suicide Cliff" because so many of the villagers had leapt to their deaths as it became apparent that the war was being controlled by the Americans.[8]

The next day I went topside very early in the morning and found that more ships had arrived during the night. Then it dawned on me that there were ships as far as I could see: battlewagons, aircraft carriers, LSTs (landing ships, tank). Name it and it was there! It was Halsey's Fleet, the most impressive sight I have ever laid eyes on.[9] In the dim light of dawn, Morse-code messages flickered between craft in the convoy. It was like a visual rendition of "The Star-Spangled Banner" from the very heart of America! A lump filled my throat, and only now will I admit to a tear or two.

Departing Saipan, we seemed to be at sea for a long time, but it was not all boring. We got a good look at a school of whales, detonated loose mines in the water, learned some Japanese from a backwoods sergeant from Kentucky, and watched a Marine colonel throw a side of spoiled beef with a surprise in it over the fantail. The colonel had a very long cord attached to the pin of a hand grenade inside the meat. As we sailed away, several sharks began to chow down on the meat. When the cord ran out, the pin was pulled from the grenade, and dinner was à la flambé. At least one shark got a bad case of heartburn.

To entertain ourselves, we pulled a lot of pranks. One was very familiar to anyone who has ever been aboard a crowded troop transport. The head (bathroom) had two long water troughs that extended down both sides of the ship's hull. There was a constant flow of water at all times. Appropriate seats were placed along the top of the trough as the water passed rapidly underneath. The trick was to get the first seat upstream and be prepared to make a quick exit after lighting a flotilla of toilet tissue. It would send a warm, cheery flame under the bare exposed parts of preoccupied men. If you were nimble enough, you wouldn't get caught.

All fun ceased when our entire convoy got caught in a typhoon that had made an unexpected turn into the China Sea. Imagine the entire bow of a very large ship completely submerged in water right up to the ship's superstructure. I just knew that we were done for. All sorts of rumors went around, such as the possibility that some of the smaller vessels in our convoy had been sunk. We did see the ship behind us get off course and almost ram our fantail. That would have been curtains! I suppose that the worst part of the storm was the seasickness. If you didn't get sick from the storm, you would be from the stench of everyone else getting sick.[10]

At last we sighted the dim outline of mountains, then thousands of little islands protruding up in very high knolls of bright green vegetation. Occasionally, there was some sign of life, such as a shack or a small boat moored near the base of the island. What couldn't be seen was any living soul. We did see several bodies afloat. They were assumed to be suicide victims who had committed *hara-kiri* because of Japan's surrender.

Our ship slowed to a crawl as we were met by a Japanese tug, which guided us through narrow passages into the Port of Sasebo on the western tip of Kyushu, Japan.[11] There were a number of cargo vessels sunk in the harbor. We went ashore in Higgins boats (landing craft). The infantry went a different route, through marsh up to their waists. So far, not a shot had been fired.

We landed in a small clearing of solid ground. As we were going ashore, we saw two or three Higgins boats loaded with men who appeared to have come out of an old folks' home: gaunt, dirty—and lucky. These were the POWs who had survived while two-thirds of their original number had died from starvation, disease, and torture.[12] They were waving, crying, and yelling in disbelief. Seeing the end of their ordeal made all the blood of battle worthwhile. We never forgot what they looked like coming out of the concentration camps. It made us realize that combat troops turned occupation troops were really not the best means for teaching the Japanese justice for all under the democratic system. We had been fighting these people. We could not just flip a switch and turn off all the instincts of battle. Hate was very deep-seated and very obvious.[13]

We were ordered to check out some old barracks that must have been pre-arranged for our quarters. It was weirdly quiet there; no one was around the place, which looked as though it had been vacated a very short time before. We wondered where the hell they all were. Was this one of their tricks, or what? We posted guards everyplace that night, but there was no sign of life.

The next day, some of the high-ranking Japanese officers came into camp and announced themselves as goodwill ambassadors, but then started asking how many troops were arriving. I thought our first sergeant was going to fire them out of our howitzers! As time went by, other people began to come down from the hills. Most of them were scared civilians who had been told terrible things about American Marines.

Our new quarters in Sasebo came equipped with a squadron of fleas. They were numerically and individually huge, and they did bite. This resulted in a decontamination operation in which we wore nothing but gas masks held on with one hand. We held our clothes in the other hand while the medics hosed us down with DDT. It did the trick.

We began a routine patrol every day touring the city and waterfront, and I was back in my old Jeep, Liberty Hound. It was hard to tell whether or not the A-bomb had been dropped in Sasebo as well, because it had suffered unbelievable destruction from American bombers with apparently very precise targets. For example, several churches, hospitals, schools, and an orphanage were left standing while everything around them was leveled.

We were told that we would be moving to Nagasaki, but the area had not yet been cleared by the scientists studying the effects of the blast. Then, after six weeks or so, we started the move.

Along the way, we were stationed at a tiny coastal village. It was a mountainous area, and at the base of many of these mountains were entrances to tunnels that went on for great distances, finally connecting at what seemed to be the center of the mountain.[14] Here, there was a very large room that appeared to be a headquarters. Narrow gauge rails ran through every finger of the cave and every tunnel. Periodically along these rails were lathe or metal machines, used to manufacture torpedoes for suicide boats.

Our quarters were Japanese barracks close to the water's edge. Man-made inlets allowed small craft to come far inland, where there were small docks with barnlike covers. These housed the suicide boats, which were about forty feet long, built with marine plywood. They had no deck or cover, just a pilot control unit and two large Chevrolet engines (made in America) mounted toward the rear. Torpedo mounts on either side of the craft were designed to detonate on impact. These boats were really fast, and we had a lot of fun playing with them for a short period of time (without the torpedoes). Then came doomsday for about a hundred of our newfound toys.

It seemed like such a waste. These flat-bottomed craft could have been very useful, especially the Chevy engines that powered them. But we had our orders, so we took them out to sea about five miles, tied them together, and conducted artillery practice on them. It didn't take but a couple of hours for them all to burn and sink.[15]

Our demolition experts were having their fun, as well. A fine collection of various caliber shore battery and anti-aircraft guns were gathered in a long line near the water's edge. A charge of CD-2 (a brown substance that resembled modeling clay) was placed about halfway down the barrel of each gun, which was then fired. The resultant explosion made the guns look like an ostrich that had swallowed a large egg. After being destroyed in this manner, these guns, made of some of the finest steel available, were also dumped at sea.

CHAPTER FIVE

Good Conduct

I had already been to Nagasaki several times with the skipper, making preparations to move the troops. We joined the 2nd Marine Division. Separation of their oldest combat troops was underway for the long-awaited trip stateside. Some of these men had been in the islands for three years or more. We were all transformed from 5th Marine Division artillery men to 2nd Marine Division MPs, while the 5th Division, with men who had seen more combat than will ever be told, went home. Some of these men had been wounded in the early part of the war, patched up, and sent back to fight again. Later in the war, a wound was a ticket stateside.

In my new job as Military Police, I was made corporal of the guard, posting and relieving men on duty every four hours. Since I was inclined to be in trouble's way a lot, I never thought I would see the rank of corporal. But by this time I was among the older personnel, as replacements filled the vacancies on a daily basis. These changes made my life a lot easier. This new assignment enabled me to participate in patrols all around the Nagasaki area during the early days of occupation. Our job was to go to all of the major religious temples and collect all arms required to be turned in by the public. A 6 x 6 artillery truck followed us to these locations, where we loaded literally thousands of Samuri swords, *hara-kiri* daggers, and a few firearms. The swords were family heirlooms, some of them hundreds of years old. We could see the Japanese flinch as we threw the cutlery into the truck beds.

I took a hand-cranked siren from a bombed-out 1933 Japanese fire engine and mounted it on the front of the Liberty Hound. It came in handy whenever we were called on to break up fights outside the Slop Chute. The officer riding with me would crank the siren as I drove into the crowd. The British and the Russians, being our allies, came to see the destruction at Nagasaki, and significant numbers of both groups wound up in fights outside the Slop Chute. For some reason, we never seemed to get along with the British very well.

Many small towns around Nagasaki had an abundance of hot sulphur springs flowing from deep beneath the volcanic mountain base. These springs were put to use with the construction of large bathing pools about three feet deep. The pools were divided by a wall the same depth to separate the men's bathing area from the women's. There were no enclosures—the whole area was wide open. The old tradition of bathing outdoors in the nude was not unusual, except to the Marines, who found watching the pools to be one of their favorite pastimes. Movie attendance dropped dramatically in camp. Finally, guards were posted at the site after some goodwill ambassadors in Marine dress tried to join in this sanitation project!

The Japanese men hated us, obviously, but the women were very friendly for the most part. Japanese men showed little affection to their women, making them walk three paces behind and carry the burdens. This aloofness may have been traditional, but the Japanese girls loved the attention they received from the Americans—simple things, like holding doors open for them or assisting them up stairs. The hatred from the Japanese men intensified as their troops began to return from abroad. There were miles of lines of returning troops walking on either side of the road through the devastation that was once the proud city of Nagasaki. You could see the loathing in their eyes, and I am sure they could see it in ours, too. There were some instances of sniper fire and arson around our ammo dump, but things went well, considering. I must say, duty at remote guard posts like the airstrip and some of the caves that housed underground factories proved a spooky four hours. It was amazing to us that the Japanese government had such complete control over their people. Had the government ordered every last man to fight to the death, believe me, they would have.

The patrols in the small towns and villages were finally coming to an end. One of our last long patrols took us to places that were even on our map. We got ourselves good and lost on miles of unmarked, narrow roads that traversed rice paddy dams and wound around mountains before dead-ending in tiny villages. Most of the locals would run and hide, while others would line up and bow until we told them to knock it off. Then they would scramble to make some sort of peace offering to the first foreign soldiers they had ever seen.

The same Lieutenant Noteworthy who had been assigned to me as defense attorney for my court-martial was now on patrol with me. He had gained quite a reputation during the battle for Iwo Jima. He, with the forward observers, was under heavy mortar fire one morning. Like everyone else, they did their best to dig down in the hot sand to avoid shrapnel fragments. When the barrage subsided, Lieutenant Noteworthy discovered his hip and leg warmly drenched and began calling frantically for a corpsman. He thought he was bleeding badly, but didn't dare look. It turned out that a fragment of mortar shell had pierced his canteen. What he felt was the warm water running down his backside. You can imagine the jokes made about the lieutenant's worthiness of a Purple Heart medal for wounds received in battle!

Our normal patrol was made up of four people: I was the driver, Lieutenant Noteworthy was in charge, my good friend Private McGowan took notes, and a sergeant whose name I cannot recall was struggling with the Japanese language book so that he could interpret. On the tail end of one particular patrol, we were trying to find our way back to camp. It was getting late when we came upon another small village with a large, barnlike building. Although no one seemed to be around, we called out, hoping that someone could identify the place for us.

Finally, a lone man appeared out of nowhere, bowing and showing his teeth, and apparently very willing to help. He could not read our map, so he drew one on the ground for us and then offered us some *sake* (the traditional Japanese beverage made from fermented rice). He very graciously warmed it to the proper temperature and poured it from a very small vase into very small cups. Then he demonstrated how to sip it very slowly. He must have thought we were very crude as we downed cupfuls faster than he could warm them up. Finally he left and returned with a bottle for each of us. These we proceeded to drink cold. It was not until then that we realized that this building was where they made the stuff! He then introduced us to several girl workers who appeared out of the woodwork. Being the typical shy, blushing women, they were scared to death by this untoward invitation to join men in a social activity.

By the time Lieutenant Noteworthy decided we should leave, it was almost dark, and we could hardly see a thing. Normally, the lieutenant in charge would never have allowed any of this, but Lieutenant Noteworthy, like myself, was never going to earn the good conduct ribbon, and his only aim at this point was to get out in one piece. Discipline was not a part of his character.

Well, we climbed back into the Liberty Hound and took off. We kept driving just to keep moving, and—I don't know how—Lady Luck got us back to camp. LATE. The base had sent

more patrols out looking for us. Lieutenant Noteworthy was never assigned to another patrol.

Although we had been warned not to drink the water or eat any food that did not originate from our mess hall, this was not strictly enforced. There were a few places most of us would visit from time to time that served Japanese home brew and some sort of snacks—usually a hard, grainy biscuit. The only ill effects we suffered were cramps and severe nausea after consuming more than two of their twelve-ounce bottles of beer. Their beer tasted better than the beer we were getting, but no telling what additional ingredients were in it.

At first no one seemed to suffer from radiation poisoning. Since nothing was provided to protect us from contaminated air or soil, we assumed that we were not in danger. The first bizarre sign of illness that surfaced was sudden hair loss among the men. It came out in clumps. Then the divisional dentist began to see teeth that came loose without apparent cause. Next came severe headaches. Finally, several men died of leukemia. A friend of mine, Pfc. Morrow, suddenly started getting tired a lot. By the time he finally reported in to sick bay, he was so sick that he died within a few short weeks. Cancer of the blood was something that most of us had never heard of. An organization called the National Association of Atomic Veterans[1] was later to fight the U.S. government for years to help men who suffered from the effects of radiation poisoning. I felt at the time that Lady Luck had spared me, but years later, after medical tests, I discovered that the radiation had made me sterile.

Japan had its share of rain. We fought the rain and mud almost every week for long periods of time. One day I noticed the commanding officer of the 13th Marines (our regimental commander) riding in a Jeep with covered side doors made from plywood. This was a great idea, because you could not avoid getting splashed in a Jeep, especially when trucks passed by on the narrow, unpaved roads. So I took it upon myself to talk to the colonel's driver. He was very proud of the fact that the doors were his idea. As a matter of fact, the colonel had complimented him for using his head. I have no clue where he got the plywood, as that was not easily obtained. But this gave me the idea to construct some sort of door for my Jeep. I felt sure that my commanding officer would appreciate it, and I sure could use the protection.

There was a pile of discarded clothing outside the quartermaster's shack that I rummaged through, looking for old waterproof ponchos. I located enough material to outfit two doors. The rigid part of the doors was fashioned from steel rod about the thickness of a pencil. I bent the rod to conform to the side of the Jeep by the front seats and sewed the camouflage poncho material to the metal rod. Then I spot-welded two metal nuts to the side so that the rods would hinge, enabling the doors to swing open and shut.

This was a cool move. Captain Jeske was pleased with the idea, and some of the other Jeep drivers began duplicating it—until I was called in to report to the captain. It seems that a colonel at divisional headquarters had spotted my Jeep and demanded to know where I got the authority to affix side curtains onto a vehicle that was not meant to have them. Needless to say, I was once again in deep doo-doo, facing a possible court-martial for destruction of military clothing and attaching a welded bolt to a military vehicle. When Captain Jeske asked who had authorized it, I told him that I had merely followed the example of the regimental commander, who had doors on his Jeep.

This reasoning did not fly, so the doors came off and I was put on report. I avoided a court-martial only because a colonel had done the same thing; the difference being that his doors stayed on. Through all this, no one mentioned the siren that remained on the Jeep!

Our motor pool headquarters, where all repairs were made, was located in a huge, creaky old warehouse in which all sorts of parts had been stored for submarines, tugboats, etc. It was a sinister place in which to gas up during the middle of the night—our gasoline supply was housed inside with a single light bulb to illuminate where the fuel was located, and there was one guard posted in this enormous building. Many times, he would be making his rounds so far away that you would never see him, especially since there were so many interesting things to investigate: an old train engine and boxcars, submarine parts, and partially assembled subs in various stages of completion.

There were reports from time to time that an unauthorized person was in the building. After a while, this person became bold enough to show himself and speak to the guard in broken English. He wanted to buy American cigarettes. Someone sold them to him. Soon he brought a friend, and they began to inquire about clothing and food. The guards passed this information to each other, and the next thing you know, the spooky old warehouse turned into tradeday headquarters.

The industrious Japanese had plenty of yen, but no place to spend it. The Marines were in a similar bind: we sent most of our pay home because there was no place to spend it other than the PX (supply store) or on beer. You could not send any more money home than what you were paid. That was not much, less than $70 a month if you were a PFC.

It was not long before we had more damn money that we knew what to do with. The rate of exchange was fifteen yen (in American occupation currency, cosponsored by the American and Japanese governments) to the American dollar. You could buy a lot of Japanese beer for fifteen yen. Then, the Japanese-American business cooperative progressed a step further when the Japanese buyers were able to provide American money for their purchases. I don't know where they managed to get American currency, but it began to show up. In the meantime, we discovered that whenever our Navy pulled into port, the sailors were limited in the amount they could convert to Japanese yen from American currency. Apparently this was not enough, because they drank oceans of beer, and if they toured the area where the girls were, they needed even more yen.

Thank goodness for the helpful Marines who came to their rescue and gladly supplied them with all of the exchange they could afford! This went on for a long time, until some officer from division headquarters noticed that Japanese men were looking more American and, in some cases, better dressed than the American military.

Threatening memos came down from headquarters with nothing less than a general court-martial for anyone caught selling GI anything, including cigarettes (50¢ a carton to us from the PX, and $5 to the buyer). Shoes were very much in demand, but Japanese feet were so small that American shoes wouldn't fit them, for the most part.

Well, the crackdown began. When our new clothing issue was drastically reduced, a lot of us were going practically naked. You couldn't buy a candy bar at the PX for a long time. Tragically, our supply of items like this was reduced to nothing, thus ending a very enterprising business endeavor.

Cpl. David Milam after the change from artillery man to Military Police in Nagasaki. The hand-cranked siren can be seen mounted on the right edge of the windshield. Theoretically, he should have been court-martialed for the unauthorized fixture, but none of the officers he drove cared to make an issue of it (as they had the doors).

Cpl. David Milam in a rickshaw (jinrikisha). This was the only form of taxi transportation available.

Photo of Japanese sailor found in the barracks at Sasebo. As a joke, Milam had noted on the back, "Just thought I would send you this picture of my top sarge."

Entrance from the Sea of Japan into Nagasaki Bay. Note the sunken vessel to the right of the island in center of picture.

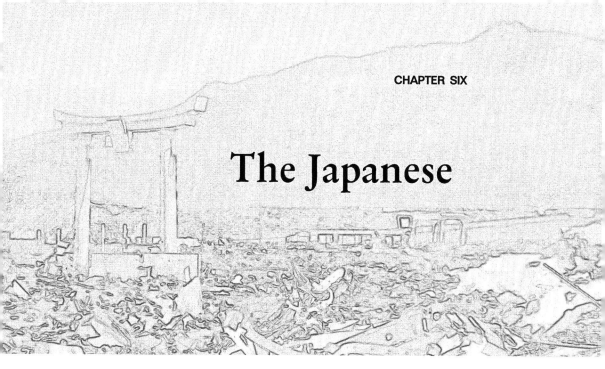

CHAPTER SIX

The Japanese

Guard duty now replaced patrols. It was boring until our long-lost sea bags mysteriously arrived from somewhere. I had taken a big chance on stashing that old box camera in my sea bag. But the good conduct medal was something that I had already lost during the first six months of my career as a Marine. At Nagasaki, NO PHOTOS was definitely engraved in stone. A court-martial was in store for souvenir hunters and photographers. Headquarters kept the bomb site off-limits until all bodies could be removed from the debris, which took months. The stench of the dead was so overwhelming that you could never become accustomed to it. It even lingered in our clothes. Under the ruins of rubble and waste were body parts and burned flesh, the smell of which subsided only after the winter months offered Mother Nature's cleansing touch.

Even places outside of Nagasaki smelled terrible because of the open sewage. The locals thought nothing of relieving themselves whenever and wherever they felt the urge. Every inch of the

countryside was farmed, even the mountainsides, which looked like a quilted work of art on a grand scale. Unfortunately, the country smelled as bad as the city because farms were fertilized with human manure. This was accomplished by hundreds of men we called "honey dippers." Each day they would run in a short, choppy trot shouldering their burden—a long pole narrowed at the ends, on which hung wooden buckets filled with liquid human fertilizer obtained from huge cesspools. Since the poles were limber, the short trot allowed a kind of rhythm and balance. These frail little men would go for miles on their appointed rounds. Why disease did not destroy them all, I'll never know. Later I learned that these pathetic people were slaves from other countries such as China and Korea.[1]

One Sunday morning, when most of us could relax and do what we wanted, a public relations officer came into our quarters looking for a volunteer to chauffeur a Jesuit priest around to various locations. The driver would be given the freedom to go anyplace, even to restricted and off-limits areas. That sounded interesting, so I volunteered.

The priest I had volunteered to drive was an Italian who spoke seven languages well. He had been assigned to the Catholic Church of Layan for a number of years, but had been sent to Kobe on a new assignment sometime prior to the bomb drop. Much as I've tried, I cannot recall his name. I guessed him to be around forty-five years old.

Every Sunday thereafter, he requested me to drive him, and that is how I learned what I did about the Japanese culture and centers. We became friends, but he always kept his distance. He was preoccupied much of the time. There was no question that he was very much opposed to the bomb drop, as he cherished these people. I met quite a few important people while ferrying him around, and he never failed to introduce me as his friend.

We attended many political and informational meetings regarding the U.S. government's plans for various aspects of reconstruction, such as the freeing of slaves, punishment of war atrocities, and distribution of food to the population.[2] Many business leaders and people of importance attended these meetings— among them was Mr. Okabe, a respected man of means. His family owned the Okabe Department Store in Nagasaki, which escaped destruction.

I accompanied the Jesuit priest to the Okabe home, and while he and Mr. Okabe were in conference, I was introduced to his daughters Kimiko and Kiyoka. As they were studying English, conversation came easily. I was the first American GI that had passed muster to meet them, thanks to the padre's introduction.

After that, I was invited back to have dinner with them, and returned for many more visits. The girls were very polite, and anxious to further their knowledge of English.[3] In return, they explained subtleties of their culture and way of life that I never would have grasped on my own. They were somewhat bitter about the blast, but not toward me as an individual, more toward the U.S. government. As we talked, it became apparent that they had been fed a string of lies about the reasons for the war, about Pearl Harbor. Little by little, they came to accept what I told them as the truth.

I was surprised to see that even the well-to-do like the Okabes were short of many necessities. I became a real hero when I showed up at their home one morning with a fifty-pound sack of sugar under the tarp in the back seat of my Jeep. The cooks and messmen are still trying to figure out where that went.

Later, when time came for me to go home, the Okabes presented me with Kiyoka's original artwork and a fan with the rising sun on it from Kimiko. We corresponded for several years after that.[4]

While on solo missions around the bomb site, I observed so many remarkable things that I decided to take pictures, regardless of the threats. Miraculously, my parents' old box camera had survived its wanderings with minimal damage, only slightly skewed. So I straightened it out and wrapped it up with electrical tape, then carried it with me on patrols. I kept it hidden in a locked compartment beside the wheel well in the Jeep, where the jack normally went. I also took a few articles that could be hidden from inspection, among them some Japanese coins partially melted by the atomic heat. But since I did not care to spend time in a Marine Corps brig, my record-keeping activities were kept to a minimum during the six months I was there.

The submarines still on the production line at the demolished Mitsubishi plant fascinated me, mainly because of what I had heard. Scuttlebutt around the Marine Corps was just that—gossip—but sometimes it seemed more accurate than what was posted on the bulletin board. One kid from the Galveston Bay area told us stories of Japanese subs surfacing at night to shell the Sinclair storage tanks, starting fires that destroyed precious fuel. I was not sure how accurate this could be, since there was never anything on the news about it.

Years after the war, around 1947, I was employed by the Atlantic Refinery Company as a land surveyor. We surveyed the company's oil lease boundaries, placed markers at drill sites, and so forth. On one occasion, we were working on a number of small islands just off Galveston, Texas—Mustang Island among them. Some of them were so small, we could wade from island to island. On this particular day, I noticed a fifty-five-gallon barrel that had washed ashore. It was pretty rusty, and covered with Japanese writing. Later, I found a tennis shoe. Not just any shoe, but one that I instantly recognized as Japanese in origin, for theirs were made to encase the big toe separately from the other toes. I wondered about this for a long time. Years later, an ex-Navy fighter pilot named Barney Broyles told me that when he was in training at the Naval Air Station in Corpus Christi, enemy subs were sighted from time to time in the shallow waters off our coast.[5]

While in Nagasaki, I also had occasion to explore the shell of the medical center that stood there. Although the building stood, the interior was totaled—no wood or fabric. Beds and gurneys were a mass ot twisted steel. Nothing was left of windows or frames. I walked up a cement staircase that led to what I assumed was a storage area. From there, all glass containers had melted and run down the steps like molten lava. On one wall close to a window, the outline of a person was clearly visible, imprinted on the wall by the blast. I could not photograph it, because there were other officers with me at the time.[6]

There were funerals every day. Some days the funeral processions seemed endless. And I saw a few survivors of the blast. The memory of one man in particular stands out—one side of his face was burned badly, the other was normal. On the burned side of his body, the skin that was protected by clothing was a different texture than the rest of his skin. His wide belt had protected a swath around his waist, as his shoes had protected his feet.

One thing I never understood was the apparent coldness of the Japanese culture toward their own people. The only mass transit out of the city was the train. The tracks were made functional fairly easily since they offered no vertical resistance to the bomb, and all that needed repair were the wooden ties. Still, it took months to complete. The train ran either north or south on certain days. It did not run often, nor even every day. Hundreds of people would walk for miles to the station and wait for days before space was available on the train. As a result, there were always people camping along the tracks. None could be seen shedding a single tear even under the most trying conditions. Many times along the road we would see a man or woman who could not go any farther because of injury or illness. They were just left there as others passed them by with no indication of concern. The only help they got was when one of our trucks or Jeeps would stop and take them to the overcrowded hospital. We did not know for a long time that the hospitals were controlled by the government, and the only people admitted were those of some importance. When the doctors tried to turn away a patient we had brought in, we threatened them within an inch of their lives. Word of this eventually got back to our Headquarters, and we were told just to leave them be.

I wondered how a nation that appeared to be so poor and backward could dream of conquering the United States! The bicycle was the only mode of transportation for most people, other than walking, and many people walked in thongs made of old tire tread. To fish, they would hold a small, glass-bottomed box in one hand to peer down into the water, then, with the other, spear small fish they found. These they would string up on drying racks and use in soup. I couldn't understand how they could eat it, because it smelled so bad! Still, they were very clean people who lived in the midst of filth. It was apparent that every resource they possessed had gone for supporting their military.

There seemed to be a lot of Japanese women with tiny babies. They carried them on their backs all day long, even on work details in the hot sun. I have seen pictures of American Indian squaws carrying their papooses in the same fashion: on a cloth-covered board, facing out. It looked extremely uncomfortable for the child, being lashed to a board for such long periods of time. One very noticeable result of this custom was the flattening of the babies' heads. It gave rise to the epithet of "slope heads" or "gooks." While these words are considered terribly offensive today, it was a different world fifty years ago.

I had the good fortune to meet an eighty-two-year-old man named Edward Zilling. He was born an American citizen and had served in the Marine Corps at the turn of the century. In 1927 he moved to Nagasaki and married a Japanese girl, with whom he raised a family. When the war came, he was imprisoned in a concentration camp in Nagasaki. He said the mistreatment he suffered made the years there very hard for him. I find it interesting that today our government is roundly condemned for the internment of the Japanese living in America during the war, while the reverse is never mentioned.[7]

Prior to the invasion of Japan, the Japanese government had established what they called "comfort houses," in which girls were forced into prostitution for the pleasure of the soldiers. Some of the women were daughters of farmers who were unable to come up with their quota of produce for the government. They were required to make up the difference with income that the daughter would earn. Some were from other Oriental countries, especially China. They may have been enslaved. I am not clear on that arrangement, except that the Japanese detested the Chinese.

There were two entire districts where these women were housed. They were called *Issumachi* and *Marimachi* (*machi* meant "street"). There must have been hundreds of these women in each district. According to what I learned, they were indoctrinated to believe that their service was an honor in that it aided the war effort of the Imperial Army and Navy, and there was nothing shameful about it. After the invasion, the houses continued to operate, and U.S. servicemen began to frequent them. Without knowing then how the women felt about their "service," I did observe how delighted they were to be mistaken for geishas by the foreigners. Geishas were not prostitutes—they were educated, well-trained entertainers and hostesses, and the comfort girls did not object to the label.

Later, bowing to ugly realities, our government took over and restricted these women for U.S. servicemen only. This, along with medical examinations and treatment for the women, was to prevent the spread of disease to our troops. Guard duty in these areas was heavy as various ships came into Nagasaki from other allied countries. As MPs, our job was to patrol these areas. The women in charge of these houses— "Mamasans," we called them—would anxiously ask us about rumors they had heard to the effect that MacArthur was coming to close them down.

Finally, toward the end of my stay at Nagasaki, our government stood up to the Japanese who were opposed to closing the comfort houses (thus losing the revenue) and ordered the women freed

with some amount of compensation. This was the first time that I saw any of these women shed tears. Some of our troops were teary-eyed, as well.[8]

Around the latter part of June 1946, our tour of duty came to an end. General MacArthur's troops were beginning to spill in by the thousands. They were all decked out in dress uniforms and shiny boots, with silk scarves around their necks. Their vehicles were without camouflage, and their helmets shone with chrome plate. They even had a division band that played as they marched through the main square. They made us look like orphans! They also had the *Corps du Prix*, a French citation given to their unit during World War I. It was a braided sash worn on the left shoulder of the dress uniform. Under the circumstances, we felt compelled to inform the Japanese that these sashes served as a warning that the wearer was infected with a social disease. It was our swan song. *Sayonara!* Good-bye!

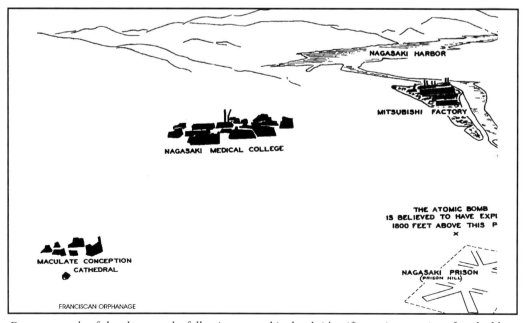

Drawn to scale of the photo on the following page, this sketch identifies major remains after the blast. The sketch was taken from "Pictorial Arrowhead: Occupation of Japan by Second Marine Division."

"Valley of Death" — Nagasaki after the blast. This photo and the sketch preceding it were taken from a memory book prepared for the Marines following the occupation titled, *" Pictorial Arrowhead: Occupation of Japan by Second Marine Division."*

Children in a Nagasaki storefront. The child in front is standing on the edge of an open sewer.

Private First Class McGowan took this photo of Corporal Milam, who is standing over the remains of someone's sole means of transportation. The hospital is in the background.

Nagasaki's largest medical center (which was government-supported) was located on the edge of the blast area. The building stood, an empty shell. In the foreground is the archway leading to a Buddhist or Shinto temple. The entire area reeked of decaying human flesh buried under tons of debris.

Partial view of blast site with hospital on far left (a modern structure of steel and concrete) and the Church of the Immaculate Conception on the right (also of strong construction). Small businesses and/or homes had existed in between. Note the open sewer in the immediate foreground.

This automobile had been someone's prized possession. It looked like a 1933 Ford Coupe that had been garaged in an upscale neighborhood. Cars were rare in Japan, as they could only be maintained by the very wealthy. Since no gasoline was readily available, all cars had been converted to run on ethanol. They sounded like the "African Queen" and had very little horsepower.

Graveyard of the Catholic Church. Although it does not show up in the photo, there was a residual shadow on the wall of a person standing nearby when the blast hit. In the center foreground is a grave marker.

Private First Class McGowan stands in front of the ruins of the Catholic Church of Layan (also called the Church of the Immaculate Conception). Run by the Jesuit order, it had been the largest church in Japan, with over ten thousand parishioners.

Ruins of the Catholic church.

A third view of the church.

Taken from the Central Police Station (the prison) looking down at what had been the center of the Nagasaki business district and the sprawling Mitsubishi plant (with smokestacks). The atomic bomb was ignited 1,650 feet directly over this area. Three square miles were so demolished that Marine bulldozers cleared the ground for a small landing strip, and later, a baseball diamond. In the foreground is the main road into the city.

View from photo on bottom of previous page is reversed, looking up toward the police station where main police operations were directed. This included interrogations of American POWs, most of whom were pilots shot down during air strikes over the city. This building had a basement where prisoners were said to have been kept at the time of the bomb drop. Milam's search there for dog tags or some confirming ID yielded nothing.

Main plant headquarters of Mitsubishi, located along the waterfront and shipping docks. Pior to the bomb drop, this building was hit by American aircraft, possibly a dive bomber. It must have been a carefully selected target as the result of intelligence efforts.

The Mitsubishi plant. These huge, steel-framed buildings housed the production of bearings, casting of engine parts, etc. The sheet metal that had covered the buildings had all been blown off. Pieces were found miles away throughout the countryside. Notice how the steel skeletons lean to the left, away from the center of the blast. The hillsides in the background were laid bare where the furnace-like wind was funneled up; on the opposite side of the mountains, most greenery was undisturbed. Two figures can be seen here: one near the center, and one to the right of center. Milam often saw people at the sites praying, scavenging, or just trying to locate where a particular building once stood. The twisted tubular frame in the right foreground was either a hand-drawn two-wheel cart or a rickshaw.

Taken from the roof of the barracks. Shown are Japanese ships in Nagasaki Bay and the city on the far side. Behind Milam was the Mitsubiship plant. The mountains, denuded on this side by the blast, channeled the force of the blast up and away from the residential area on the other side of the mountain.

A two-man submarine still on the assembly line at the Mitsubishi plant launch site. German submarines had worked their way into the Gulf of Mexico near Corpus Christi, Texas, during the early part of the war. It was Milam's understanding that the first Japanese prisoner of war was taken from a submarine like this that had become beached at Pearl Harbor.

Tug boat blown in half while tied up at the Mitsubishi docks. It had been destroyed by American aircraft some time before the bomb drop, and was removed from the water to make room for other vessels. Milam asked the mother and daughter why they were going through the debris, but could not understand their explanation.

CHAPTER SEVEN

Homeward Bound

Only problem was, I wasn't going anywhere! I had to serve more time because of my court-martial. We were sent home according to how many points we had, based on years of service, combat time, overseas duty, etc. My little visit to the brig cost me about six points. This system was created because there were just not enough guys to maintain the Military Police until the Army took over.

I became bitter. All of my old pals were going home, and just a few like me were left. After a little while, though, things began to look up. Knowing the ropes paid off. I discovered there was a rest camp for those who could show they had put in at least eighteen months overseas. It was an old vacation resort about one hundred miles away (by twisting, mountainous roads) called Obama. It was great: no roll call; the best food I'd had in a long time; hot sulphur baths; massages any time; fishing from nice boats that had been confiscated from high-ranking Japanese officers; and beautiful surroundings. These vacations were for seven days at a time. With all the

confusion going on and replacements coming in, I put in for—and received—three vacations in a row. I began to feel like a civilian again. Then, after my last vacation, I was told a new assignment was awaiting me. I was sure that meant only one thing: trash detail.

My new assignment was to join a party of twenty men at a location near Obama. We were to act as guards on a work detail that involved destroying all sorts of ammo and explosives that had been hidden in caves. Not only that, but we were to hire locals to do all of the manual labor. There was no limit on how many we could hire and no directives as to what their exact jobs would be. So we hired most of them to do the job, but we also hired people to supply fish, cook for us, wash our clothes, and clean our quarters. The place was a fairyland! The lieutenant in charge was never there, and when he was around, he didn't seem to care what we did. We became great friends with the Japanese. The only inconvenience I suffered was that the lieutenant took Liberty Hound whenever he left. Still, we had transportation: four 6 x 6 trucks, as I recall.

The caves had narrow rails that carried little flatcars, which were powered by hand. The locals loaded the ammo, consisting of hand grenades and anti-aircraft shells, into the cars and wheeled them out for disposal under our supervision. We started out by the book, carrying carbine rifles and carefully supervising the locals, for they could have definitely finished us if any of them decided to rekindle the war. But they appeared docile and happy, never showing any signs of hostility, probably because they had never left Japan, either being too young or too old to fight.

Sergeant Miller, who had decided to make a career of the Marine Corps, and I were the only people with rank above private. We had control of the operation all to ourselves with the exception of our never-there lieutenant and an occasional visit from some major whom we were supposed to report to.

We employed a Japanese fisherman who owned a small barge. It, like every other skiff or sampan, was powered by a long paddle that was lashed to the rear of the craft and worked back and forth in a U motion. Skillfully done, it was amazing to watch. We loaded shells and warheads on the barge, took them out to sea, and dumped them. Dynamite and other explosives were stacked in a low area and burned.

After a while, we became complacent, using our rifles for target practice. We let the Japanese shoot, too. It became rare for anyone to carry a weapon on a work detail. One great sport was to go out in the small fishing boats and drop hand grenades into the water. The explosion sent up a column of water ten or fifteen feet in the air, along with fish that floundered to the surface. Sometimes

there would be several boats in the water. We found great pleasure in quietly dropping a grenade in the path of the boat behind us. It resulted in their getting a good bath and our receiving a good cussing out. We had to quit it when the boat owners complained that the shock waves were causing their craft to leak.

Thing were going so well that we decided to slow down a little, as we were not anxious to see this demolition job end any too soon. At this point, we discovered an old vault at the dead end of one of the caves. It was American-made, and locked—but not for long. With the wide selection of explosives we had on hand, we easily removed the door. The safe contained small silver bars weighing a few pounds at most. Everybody got at least one bar and was sworn to secrecy. The safe and its door were dumped in the sea. Some of the men were afraid that if they got caught going home with contraband, they would be jailed. So they passed their bars on to others who were willing to risk it. I wound up having silver trinkets made from the bars so that they would pass as purchased items.

One bright morning as we were finishing a great breakfast, a Jeep drove up. The driver had orders to bring three of us, myself included, back to the base in Nagasaki, preparatory to returning stateside. We were going home! Of course, I wanted to go home, but I had mixed emotions. I had rather gotten to like things here.

The men under us and the Japanese workers gave us a farewell party that consisted of beer and *sake*, cookies and treats. Even the lieutenant was there. The Japanese sang a song to say *sayonara*, good-bye. At the time, it sounded very pretty. I even thought the high-pitched string instruments nice. My head was swimming.

Back in Nagasaki headquarters, I appreciated even more what a great deal that demolition detail had been. Regimentation and all of that *Gung Ho* crap was really hard to get used to again after almost two months of freedom.

I assumed that we were to leave immediately for Sasebo to ship out. It was not until we were all loaded in trucks that we were told our trip home would be delayed a few days because of an epidemic of sleeping sickness in and around Nagasaki. We would take a side trip to Saga, a little town about twenty-five miles from Sasebo.

Despite our disappointed griping, we soon arrived at Saga, where we would be housed in old Japanese barracks that were being readied for U.S. Army troops scheduled to arrive as soon as we left. Saga was much higher in altitude than anywhere else we had been stationed, which made the air a little better, at least.

At Saga, we were in for an ordeal, specifically, vaccinations. The day after we arrived, an open barracks was made ready, and we all lined up to receive our sleeping sickness shots. As I stood in line, I watched the men ahead of me lurch away in pain after being vaccinated. When my turn came, I watched the corpsman fill the syringe with a milky substance as thick as syrup. Once he plunged the needle into my arm, he had to use both thumbs to empty the syringe. It left a huge knot which he swabbed it with iodine. He told me to massage it vigorously to work the serum into the tissue. I took three steps and then felt an invisible horse kick me in the arm. It made me and almost everybody else half sick, so that we skipped chow call that evening.

For the next two days I prearranged to paint my arm with iodine before I got in line for shots. Then, in the confusion of guys horsing around in line, I took my jacket half off and walked past the officer in charge rubbing my arm, as if I had just received the shot. Still, my arm was sore for days afterward. I was convinced that sleeping sickness could not have been as bad as those shots.

Next on the agenda was to turn in our rifles, bayonets, and helmets. This disappointed me, as I had really wanted to abscond with my artillery and helmet without chancing another court-martial. So I buried my helmet deep in my seabag and accidentally picked up some junior second lieutenant's helmet, which I turned in as my own. I grudgingly handed over my rifle as well.

For the next ten days or so, we sat around recuperating from our shots, playing poker, sleeping, and wondering why we weren't shipping out. We were precision marching, however, and we had to sing the little songs as we marched, like, "Oh, how we love the Saga kin, I hope we don't return again," and, "We heard this was a mechanized war, what the hell are we marching for? One, two, three, four, one two." It was disgusting—as if we would certainly hate it if we forgot how to march.

When the big day finally arrived, we were sent to Sasebo, Japan, for debarkation. We were to board the USS *Ernie Pyle*, a liberty ship commissioned after the famous war reporter who was killed during the invasion of Okinawa. As we boarded ship, a crowd gathered, and by that afternoon there were literally hundreds of Japanese *coybitos* (sweethearts) frantically waving good-bye, sobbing after "Bobbysan," "Jimmysan," or "Charlesson." Some of them even tried to board ship, thinking they would be permitted to join their supposed fiancés.

We set sail the early part of July 1946. It seemed strange to be really going home. The USS *Pyle* was the best ship that I ever had the good fortune to board. Everything was great until some dumb officer got the idea that we should have rifle inspection. It must have been intended as a reminder that we weren't home yet. It was double trouble for me, because I had filled my barrel with pearls that I had gotten from the Japanese fishermen while on demolition detail. We had heard talk of inspections at the docks in San Diego, and how some men had received courts-martial for possessing contraband—but here we were, mid-ocean! Needless to say, I was nervous, even though I had come by the pearls honestly. So, as inspection got underway, I hastily removed the cap from the rifle barrel and emptied the pearls into a sock, which I wadded up and stuffed in my knapsack. The camera and film were in my seabag, deep in the ship's hold.

Our ship finally landed at the Naval docks in San Diego. Fortune smiled on me yet again—there was no inspection. But there was a surprising number of people waiting to greet us. My heart was pumping and everyone was grinning. We were all in line to depart, and as we did, it was customary to salute the ship's flag. A colonel was standing there to supervise these salutes. He was a real jerk, making most of us salute two or three times until he thought we'd got it right.

The Marine Corps base in San Diego was spit and polish. We were housed in nice quarters and treated like celebrities. What could it mean? Well, for one thing, we were quarantined, being psychoanalyzed for "maladjustment," as well as being checked for any foreign diseases!

During this period of about two weeks we were given such excellent treatment because they were trying to encourage us to reenlist. They had special recruitment films and speeches by high-ranking officers—even a general! Ninety-nine percent of the men were not the least bit impressed. All we wanted was to go home. Then, on the last day, a full colonel was interviewing us one on one. I couldn't believe my ears when he asked, "Why would you not care to reenlist?" He even offered to give each of us an automatic promotion to the next rank. They were desperate for men to train new recruits, and when so many men refused to rejoin, it left them far short in the number required to bring them up to full strength.

July 25, 1946, I was out of there, just two days after my twenty-first birthday. Now that I could legally buy a drink, I did, with my friend Kenneth Strand, who had joined us from the original 2nd Marine Division. We went to Santa Monica Beach the next day, and took a look at Hollywood. Then we "hooked 'em" home by a two-day train ride.

My family was waiting for me.

Looking up to the temple from the steps.

This is the gateway to a temple located on the top of a high hill that overlooks the city of Nagasaki. In the foreground is the typical dress that women wore on special occasions.

Corporal Milam standing on the steps of a temple in residential Nagasaki, an area unaffected by the blast. A denuded section of the mountain can be seen in the top left-hand corner.

This was an unusual sight: Japanese women in Western-style dress. In all probability, they had adopted the dress to please certain American GIs. Post-war construction is going on in the background.

Corporal Milam and the Okabe sisters, Kiyoka (left, who signed her name "Akira" on the art work given to Milam) and Kimiko, whose family owned and operated the Okabe Department Store in Nagasaki. Their home and business were spared destruction from the bomb, as they were both located on the side of the mountain away from the blast.

Akira (Kiyoko) Okabe's drawing of Mt. Hikosan in Nagasaki, showing its face denuded by the atomic bomb blast.

Corporal Milam and Private First Class McGowan at Nagasaki headquarters immediately prior to departure stateside.

Endnotes

Chapter One

1. Milam's 5th Marine Division was activated November 11, 1943. Howard M. Conner, *The Spearhead: The World War II History of the 5th Marine Division* (Washington, D.C.: Infantry Journal Press, 1950), p. 1. This is an incredibly comprehensive history of the division's personnel and activity, including photographs. Camp life at Pendleton is memorably depicted in Lt. Robert L. Jones, ed., *The Spearhead*, 5th Marine Division, Camp Joseph H. Pendleton. (Los Angeles: Public Relations Section of the USMC, 1944).

2. Blackie Sherrod, "Code Talkers shouldn't be forgotten," *Dallas Morning News*, February 26, 1998. The Suribachi message is rendered less colorfully but probably more accurately by code talker Teddy Draper in Sally McClain's *Navajo Weapon*: "1st Lieutenant H.G. Schrier's platoon raised U.S. flag and secured Mount Suribachi at 10:20." (Boulder, Colorado: Books Beyond Borders, 1994), p. 179.

3. William Miller, "Talk Navajo," *Vantage* (Jan.-Feb. 1995): 14-15, 48.

Chapter Two

1. How Lt. Col. Evans S. Carlson treated his Raiders, and why they fought so full-heartedly for him, is described by code talker Wilsie Bitsie in McClain's *Navajo Weapon*: "'I'd watch the way he talked, the way he gave orders. Orders that took precedence were indicated by a slight raise in the tone of his voice. I never heard him yell, swear or lose his temper. If there was a group of men that were ragged, not seeming to be getting very far in their training, but ready to fight, I would hear him calmly point out what they were doing wrong and how to fix it. Then, in the same manner, he would talk to a more advanced group. No difference! I learned a lot from him, just like I did from my elders. I learned how to help, how to get along with people, to know what the word "love" is. . . . Carlson had that, and that is why I was seldom afraid during the war'" (p. 74).

2. The first phase of the assault on Guam took place between July 21 and 28, 1944: "Once ashore on the Asan beaches, the 20,000 men of the 3rd Marine Division found themselves in a precarious situation between the two 'devil's horns' (Asan and Adelup Points), the deep blue sea, and a semicircle of hills. . . . The beachhead was so covered with troops that almost every

projectile dropped into it by the enemy inflicted casualties. . . . This first week ashore had been costly for the Division. A large majority of its total casualties for the operation . . . were then incurred." Samuel Eliot Morison, *History of United States Naval Operations in World War II*, vol. VIII: *New Guinea and the Marianas* (Boston: Little, Brown and Company, 1964), pp. 386-89. Milam was probably seeing casualty lists from Saipan (June 21–July 9: 16,525 casualties) and Tinian (July 24–Aug. 1: 2,205 casualties) as well as Guam (July 21–Aug. 10: 7,083 casualties). Morison, *New Guinea and the Marianas*, pp. 339, 369, 401.

Chapter Three

1. The Marines' August 1942 invasion of Guadalcanal in the Solomon Islands was the first American offensive of the war.

2. Milam's division was among those that shipped out August or September 1944. Conner, *History of the 5th Marine Division*, p. 18.

3. On the morning of December 7, 1941, a contingent of hundreds of Japanese bomber planes attacked Pearl Harbor in the most successful surprise attack in history. In less than two hours, they had destroyed or seriously damaged 347 planes and 18 ships of war. American casualties, including civilians, totaled 3,581. See Arthur Zich, *The Rising Sun* (Alexandria, Virginia: Time-Life Books, 1977), p. 57. President Franklin D. Roosevelt, citing the "date which will live in infamy," persuaded Congress to declare war on Japan the next day. See also Gordon W. Prange, *At Dawn We Slept* (New York: McGraw Hill, 1981).

4. The taking of Tarawa in the Gilbert Islands was the first major objective of Admiral Nimitz's island-hopping campaign toward Japan. It took three days in November 1943 and cost the U.S. 3,110 in casualties. (*World Book Encyclopedia*, s.v. "World War II: The War in Asia and the Pacific," by Theodore Ropp.)

5. Tokyo Rose was actually Iva D'Aquino, a college-educated American. Following the war, she was convicted of treason, then pardoned in 1977 by President Gerald R. Ford. She claimed the Japanese forced her to make the broadcasts (*World Book*, s.v. "World War II: Psychological Warfare").

6. Due to the misleading Japanese propaganda about the progress of the war, "[t]he older Japanese on Oahu, who could not understand English, believed even after the end of the war that Japan had won, and scores of them assembled one day on Aiea Heights to see the victorious Imperial Fleet enter Pearl Harbor." War Research Lab. Univ. of Hawaii Report no. 8 of March 1, 1946; Y. Kimura, "Rumor among the Japanese," *Social Process in Hawaii* XI (1947): 84-92, quoted in Samuel Eliot Morison, *History of United States Naval Operations in World War II*, vol. XIV: *Victory in the Pacific 1945* (Boston: Little, Brown and Company, 1960), p. 351.

Chapter Four

1. The taking of Iwo Jima is commemorated in Capt. Robert L. Jones, ed., *The Spearhead*, no. 2, Iwo Jima Edition, 5th Marine Division (Los Angeles: Public Relations Section of the USMC, 1945).

2. Morison, *Victory in the Pacific*, p. 69. The Seabees—construction battalions of the U.S. Navy—were widely famed for their ability to construct or repair anything with anything.

3. Germany surrendered on May 7, 1945.

4. The "Little Boy," with a core of uranium 235, was dropped over Hiroshima on August 6, 1945. The more sophisticated and more deadly "Fat Man" was dropped over Nagasaki three days later. The bomb—ten feet long, five feet wide, 10,000 pounds, with plutonium at its core—was originally destined for Kokura, but the city was obscured by smoke or fog. The pilot, Maj. Charles Sweeney, decided at the last moment on the Mitsubishi shipyards in Nagasaki, where the torpedoes used at Pearl Harbor had been built. See Ed Timms, "Lasting im-

pact: Pilot recalls dropping atomic bomb on Nagasaki," *Dallas Morning News*, July 18, 1995.

5. "It was the Emperor who cut governmental red tape and made the great decision [to surrender]. This required courage. The Army chiefs and Admiral Toyoda were not greatly moved by the atomic explosions. They argued that the two bombs were probably all that the United States had; and if more were made we would not dare use them when invading Japan; that there was a fair chance of defeating the invasion by massed kamikaze attacks, and that in any event national honor demanded a last battle on Japanese soil.... Nothing less than an assertion of the Imperial will could have overcome these arguments and objections." Morison, *Victory in the Pacific*, p. 351. In an unprecedented move, Emperor Hirohito went on radio (in a prerecorded broadcast) to explain to his subjects: "Despite the best that has been done by everyone...the war-situation has developed not necessarily to Japan's advantage, while the general trends of the world have all turned against her interest. Moreover, the enemy has begun to employ a new and most cruel bomb...." Dan van der Vat, *The Pacific Campaign: World War II* (New York: Simon & Schuster, 1991), p. 398.

6. Milam's division shipped out for the occupation of Japan on September 1, 1945. Conner, *History of the 5th Marine Division*, p. 131.

7. Saipan is an island in the Marianas, about 1,600 miles southeast of Tokyo.

8. "A grisly postscript to the capture of Saipan was the suicide of hundreds of Japanese civilians on the northern cliffs of the island on 11 and 12 July [1944]. Rejecting invitations by the Marines to surrender, and often threatened by surviving soldiers; men, women and children cut each others' throats, deliberately drowned, or embraced death by any means they could. Parents dashed babies' brains out on the cliffs and then jumped over themselves; children tossed hand grenades to each other. This episode was a grim reminder that the road to Tokyo would still be hard and long." Morison, *New Guinea and the Marianas*, p. 338.

9. "For the actual occupation Eighth Army, lifted and supported by Admiral Halsey's Third Fleet, was assigned Honshu east of the 135th meridian; Sixth Army and Fifth Fleet took key points on western Honshu, Kyushu and Shikoku...." Morison, *Victory in the Pacific*, p. 357. Milam was sailing with the Fifth Fleet that occupied Kyushu.

10. Seaman First Class James J. Fahey described what must have been the same typhoon that Milam's ship got caught in. The storm struck September 17, 1945, when Fahey's ship, the USS *Montpelier*, was anchored in the bay near Wakayama, Japan: "A typhoon hit the harbor with winds registered as high as 125 miles per hour.... We took 38 degree rolls. The ship is constructed to take a 45 degree roll.... The water came through the ventilating system, sending water all through the ship.... Thick steel plates were bent like paper.... Large cables were broken. It was like riding a wild horse as I lay in my bunk.... Three LSTs, each 327 feet long, and a minesweeper were tossed up on the beach and against the stone cliff. They were smashed like toys." *Pacific War Diary*, 1942-1945 (Boston: Houghton Mifflin Company, 1992), pp. 392-93.

11. The American occupation fleet arrived at Sasebo, Japan, on September 22, 1945. Second Lt. Robert E. V. Johnson, ed., *The Spearhead*, vol. III, Occupation Edition (Los Angeles: Public Information Section of the USMC, 1946).

12. See Ed Timms, "'The atomic bomb saved our lives:' For U.S. prisoners of war in Japan, blast ended their misery," *Dallas Morning News*, August 13, 1995; and "Japan leader apologizes for POW treatment," *Dallas Morning News*, August 12, 1995.

13. Despite Milam's misgivings, the consensus seems to be that "on the whole the occupation proved both benevolent and

beneficial." Malcolm Kennedy, *A Short History of Japan* (New York: The New American Library, 1964), p. 293. "No other conquered people in history was treated more humanely and benefited more at the hands of its conquerors." Mikiso Hane, *Modern Japan: A Historical Survey*, 2nd ed. (Boulder, Colorado: Westview Press, 1992), p. 344.

14. Photographs of tunnels found on Kyushu can be seen in Keith Wheeler, *The Fall of Japan* (Alexandria, Virginia: Time-Life Books, 1983), p. 71.

15. On March 26, 1945, in preparation for the assault on Okinawa, U.S. infantry landing teams discovered 350 similar suicide boats (*renraku tei*) hidden among the rocky islets of the Keramas. Keith Wheeler, *The Road to Tokyo* (Alexandria, Virginia: Time-Life Books, 1979), p. 97.

Chapter Five

1. The National Association of Atomic Veterans can be located online at: http://www.aracnet.com/~pdxavets/naavsty.htm

Chapter Six

1. "Thousands of Asians had been brought to the city [Nagasaki] as slave laborers during Japan's era of colonial rule on the mainland"—and were there when the bomb was dropped. "Nagasaki observes A-bomb anniversary," *Dallas Morning News*, August 10, 1995.

2. Following the devastation of war, the Japanese people were starving. See Gwen Terasaki, *Bridge to the Sun* (Chapel Hill: Univ. of North Carolina Press, 1957). An excellent discussion of postwar reforms can be found in Chapter 15 of Hane, *Modern Japan: A Historical Survey*.

3. Some things don't change much. In a 1995 visit to Nagasaki, author Jon Krakauer noted, "It was not unusual for me to be approached on street corners— shyly, accompanied by prodigious bowing—and asked if I would mind engaging in conversation. Three times in a single afternoon I was asked by groups of gig-

gling Japanese schoolgirls if they might practice their halting English on me." "Nagasaki 50 years later," *Dallas Morning News*, March 5, 1995.

4. A letter from Kimika, dated January 11, 1949, reads in part: "We often talked about you whenever we find your picture in my album .... Two years six months have already passed since you said a good-bye to your friends in Nagasaki. How did you spend every day after those days?

    "Before three months my house moved on this address. Because that house was occupied by American government. [Milam is sure the Okabes were well compensated for it.] The house we are living in now building occupies an unrivalled situation. It has good sight and more roomy than that house .... Are you holding an office? I imagine you that get on your own red new Chevrolet. I suppose by this time you have become a complete civilian, dressed from head to toe in the most up-to-date fashion. No doubt the girls all flock after you ...."

    Kiyoka's letter, dated January 15, says in part, "What a long time since you said a good by to your little monkey in Japan. Thank you very very much for your Christmas card. We read it glad of heart. I was so glad that I forget to go to school that morning. I have been thinking of you so far from forggetting of you. I shall never forget those nice times, being very anxious to see you again .... I wish you would write to me and tell me about yourself and your country. I wanted to write you earlyer but I couln't write English letter so soon ...."

5. Twenty-four German submarines—U boats—sank fifty-six ships and damaged fourteen more in the Gulf of Mexico between 1942 and 1943. At least two Japanese men, one an officer of the Imperial Navy, were arrested in Mexico. "Galvestonians had no idea that German submarines had roamed the gulf waters almost continually until the end of 1943." From Melanie Wiggins, *Torpedoes in the*

Gulf (College Station: Texas A&M Univ. Press, 1995), front flap copy, pp. 89, 231.

6. Photographs of this shadow phenomenon at Hiroshima and Nagasaki can be seen in Wheeler, *The Fall of Japan*, pp. 142-43.

7. Of course, there were far fewer Americans in Japan than there were Japanese in America. Mr. Zilling was profiled in *The Spearhead*, vol. III, Occupation Edition. An interesting discussion of the Japanese internment in America is found in James F. Dunnigan and Albert A. Nofi, *Victory at Sea: World War II in the Pacific* (New York: William Morrow and Company, 1995), pp. 382-88.

8. See Seth Mydans, "WWII rape victim accepts Japanese reparation," *Dallas Morning News*, December 13, 1996; and "Japan's leader apologizes to women forced to be war prostitutes," *Dallas Morning News*, July 19, 1995.

Bibliography

Butow, Robert J. C. *Japan's Decision to Surrender.* Stanford: Stanford University Press, 1954.

Conner, Howard M. *The Spearhead: The World War II History of the 5th Marine Division.* Washington, D.C.: Infantry Journal Press, 1950.

Dunnigan, James F., and Albert A. Nofi. *Victory at Sea: World War II in the Pacific.* New York: William Morrow and Company, 1995.

Fahey, James J. *Pacific War Diary, 1942-1945.* Boston: Houghton Mifflin Company, 1992.

Fujita, Frank "Foo." *FOO: A Japanese-American Prisoner of the Rising Sun.* Denton, Texas: University of North Texas Press, 1993.

Hane, Mikiso. *Modern Japan: A Historical Survey.* 2nd ed. Boulder, Colorado: Westview Press, 1992.

"Japan leader apologizes for POW treatment." *Dallas Morning News.* August 12, 1995.

"Japan puzzled by war criminal crackdown." *Dallas Morning News.* December 14, 1996.

"Japan's leader apologizes to women forced to be war prostitutes." *Dallas Morning News.* July 19, 1995.

Jones, Gregg. "Film rejects casting Tojo as aggressor." *Dallas Morning News.* May 10, 1998.

———. "Bitter Plea: Women who worked as Japanese sex slaves in WWII want justice." *Dallas Morning News.* March 20, 1999.

Jones, Lt. Robert E. V., ed. *The Spearhead.* Vol. III, Occupation Edition. Los Angeles: Public Relations Section of the USMC, 1946.

———. *The Spearhead.* 5th Marine Division. Camp Joseph H. Pendleton. Los Angeles: Public Relations Section of the USMC, 1944.

———. *The Spearhead.* No. 2. Iwo Jima Edition. Los Angeles: Public Relations Section of the USMC, 1945.

Kennedy, Malcolm. *A Short History of Japan.* New York: The New American Library, 1964.

Krakauer, Jon. "Nagasaki 50 years later." *Dallas Morning News.* March 5, 1995.

McClain, Sally. *Navajo Weapon.* Boulder, Colorado: Books Beyond Borders, 1994.

Michel, Karen Lincoln. "Uncertain terms." *Dallas Morning News,* October 18, 1995.

Miller, William. "Talk Navajo." *Vantage* (Jan.-Feb. 1995): 14-15, 48.

Morison, Samuel Eliot. *History of United States Naval Operations In World War*

II. Vol. VIII: *New Guinea and the Marianas*. Boston: Little, Brown and Company, 1964.

———. *History of United States Naval Operations in World War II*. Vol. XIV: *Victory in the Pacific 1945*. Boston: Little, Brown and Company, 1960.

Mydans, Seth. "WWII rape victim accepts Japanese reparation." *Dallas Morning News*. December 13, 1996.

"Nagasaki observes A-bomb anniversary." *Dallas Morning News*. August 10, 1995.

"Nagasaki was not first target Aug. 9." *Dallas Morning News*. March 5, 1995.

Okabe, Kimika. Personal letter to David Milam. January 11, 1949.

Okabe, Kiyoka. Personal letter to David Milam. January 15, 1949.

Prange, Gordon W. *At Dawn We Slept*. New York: McGraw Hill, 1981.

Sherrod, Blackie. "Code talkers shouldn't be forgotten." *Dallas Morning News*. February 26, 1998.

Terasaki, Gwen. *Bridge to the Sun*. Chapel Hill: University of North Carolina Press, 1957.

Timms, Ed. "'The atomic bomb saved our lives:' For U.S. prisoners of war in Japan, blast ended their misery." *Dallas Morning News*. August 13, 1995.

———. "Lasting impact: Pilot recalls dropping atomic bomb on Nagasaki." *Dallas Morning News*. July 18, 1995.

———. "POW's faith in U.S. endures." *Dallas Morning News*. August 14, 1995.

van der Vat, Dan. *The Pacific Campaign: World War II*. New York: Simon & Schuster, 1991.

Webb, James. "'I Want Americans to Know the Facts:' An Interview with Retired Air Force Maj. Gen. Chuck Sweeney." *Parade*. July 30, 1995.

Wheeler, Keith. *The Fall of Japan*. Alexandria, Virginia: Time-Life Books, 1983.

———. *The Road to Tokyo*. Alexandria, Virginia: Time-Life Books, 1979.

Wheeler, Richard. *A Special Valor: The U.S. Marines and the Pacific War*. New York: Harper & Row, 1983.

Wiggins, Melanie. *Torpedoes in the Gulf*. College Station: Texas A&M University Press, 1995.

World Book Encyclopedia. S.v. "World War II: The War in Asia and the Pacific," by Theodore Ropp.

Zich, Arthur. *The Rising Sun*. Alexandria, Virginia: Time-Life Books, 1977.